How to Market Career Development Programs and Services

By Carol A. Edds

Center on Education and Work
University of Wisconsin-Madison

National Career Development Association

A founding division of the American Counseling Association

© Copyright 2008 by the National Career Development Association
   305 N. Beech Circle
   Broken Arrow, OK 74012
   Phone: (866) 367-6232
   Fax: (918) 663-7058

Library of Congress Cataloging-in-Publication Data

Edds, Carol A., 1956–
   How to market career development programs and services / by Carol A. Edds.
      p. cm.
   ISBN 978-1-885333-23-0
   1. Career development. 2. Vocational guidance. 3. Marketing. I. Title.
   HF5381.E33 2008
   331.25'920688--dc22

                              2008025052

Table of Contents

Introduction

If you are responsible for the design and delivery of career development programs and services, then you probably also are involved in the promotion of those events and services. It's also likely that your background is as an expert in some area of career development, not in marketing and promotions.

Yet, the reality is that many of us in the career development field need to know how to design programs and services that meet our audiences' needs, oversee the development of flyers, brochures, or Web sites that tell others what we do, and attract customers to our events or into our offices.

After more than 25 years as a marketing and promotional specialist in business, education, consumer, and nonprofit sectors, I have come to this conclusion: Regardless of the intended audience, the work setting, or the type of product, program, or service being offered, having an understanding of basic marketing principles and how to apply them will always result in more effective promotions. In this case, that will lead to more successful and useful career development pro-grams, products, and services. Sometimes people ask me if marketing know-how comes naturally, or if it is something that can be learned. It is my belief that the fundamental concepts of marketing can be taught to anyone who is willing to learn, and that nearly everyone can learn to effectively apply these concepts with practice.

Gaining knowledge of elemental marketing and promotional strategies, and learning how to apply them, results in cost-effective and successful marketing efforts. This monograph will address the most basic of these principles and show how they can be used in career development, career counseling, and related areas. While there are many variables that will dictate the specifics of your marketing and promotional campaigns and activities, the tips and techniques discussed in this document place emphasis on the prime concepts and proven practices that marketers have used successfully from the beginning of time up until today.

Chapter 1
What is Marketing and Why Does It Matter?

The marketing and promotion of career development programs and services is a part of service delivery in which many professionals, both veterans and newcomers, do not have formal training or experience. Yet most counselors, trainers, developers, and evaluators of career development programs and services find that they are involved in handling responsibilities that fall under the general heading of marketing or promotion at some level. In fact, marketing is a component of many of the activities career development professionals perform as part of their everyday work, whether that is planning and delivering a workshop, writing a brochure, deciding what to put on a Web site, designing a business card, or doing a wide variety of other activities that are a regular part of our jobs. By examining what marketing is, and by broadening our understanding of what makes up marketing and promotional efforts, we begin to see that everyone performs some type of marketing or promotional activity nearly every day. The way that we carry ourselves and how we present our opinions or knowledge are examples of ways that each of us is involved in personal marketing and promotion on a daily, even hourly, basis.

When exploring how to develop our skills in the marketing and promotional aspects of our work, it helps to start by considering just what marketing encompasses. In the Career Development Facilitator (CDF) competencies developed by the National Career Development Association, the marketing related competency is stated as "knowing how to market and promote career development programs with staff and supervisors." I always broaden the competency as stated to include not just staff and supervisors, but also *potential customers*. All of us, whether we are CDFs, instructors, trainers, counselors, educators, or employment specialists, are involved in the delivery of some type of service or program to *potential or current customers or clients*. These customers could be students, adults in transition, colleagues, recent graduates, new retirees, or anything in between. If there weren't any customers or clients for us to serve, we would not be in business. So reaching out to those individuals and groups about what we have available (our programs, services, and resources) is the very essence of what marketing is about. It is also the reason why sound marketing must be understood and practiced if we want to succeed.

We are going to take a look at basic concepts and strategies that can be applied to almost any marketing or promotional endeavor. Years ago, when I took my first college course in marketing, my initial thought was "This is easy! It's just common sense." Today, I'm happy to say I've seen many career practitioners come to the same realization. A lot of marketing is common sense. At the same, some individuals have a natural inclination and skills in marketing as well as an innate understanding of its underlying psychology. Yet I believe that most people can learn how to apply essential marketing tenets to develop quality programs, services, and resources to inform others about these offerings in a more efficient and cost-effective manner. Many practitioners, who are experts in their field of knowledge, lack the marketing knowledge and experience to write an effective brochure, decide who to send e-mails to about an upcoming event, or determine fees for their services. By exploring some basic marketing concepts, career development experts and novices alike will be able to address their unique marketing challenges equipped with the same tools that every "natural" marketing guru or professional marketer uses.

Three Keys: Cost, Audience, and Timing

Effective marketing can be boiled down to three simple but important guidelines. Get your message out

1. cost-effectively,
2. to the right people, and
3. at the right time.

Missing the mark on any of these three targets can lead to ineffective marketing practice, which in turn can lead to wasted time, money, and effort. To illustrate, imagine you are putting together a series of trainings related to employability skills for students at a four-year undergraduate institution. You and your team put together an informative, inexpensive, and engaging brochure and send out e-mails to all junior and senior students on campus to announce the events. Unknowingly, you send the e-mails on the last class day before spring break, announcing that the first training is scheduled the first week students are back on campus. In addition, the brochures won't be printed until halfway through spring break because the printing shop depends upon student helpers for printing jobs and the students will be off campus at the time you need the job run. Can you see how difficult it will be now to make this promotional effort—and therefore, the entire program—succeed? Even though the first two factors, *cost* and *getting to the right people*, were met, by delivering your message at the wrong time for your particular audience of students, you have missed the important factor of promoting *at the right time*.

Here's another example based on my personal experience. I once was a direct response copywriter for a major insurance corporation. (I'll explain direct response later, but for now, just know it means I created the kinds of mailings you get in your home mail designed to sell you auto or life insurance—sometimes called "junk mail.") The nice thing about direct response marketing is that you get a "direct response" from any promotional or advertising action you take, and this response is tracked so that the marketer can determine the effectiveness of the promotion. (In contrast, *general* marketing usually is part of a larger campaign, and direct results of marketing activities cannot be tracked.)

A higher level manager at the insurance company thought it would be a good idea to make insurance "personal" for our audience. He wanted us to feature one of our own lower level managers—a young, up-and-coming business man, recently married and with a new mortgage. The higher level manager asked us to write a brochure in which this young man talked one-to-one with the potential customer about his own insurance needs. Unfortunately, as sometimes happens in large corporations, the concept had not been fully developed before it was passed on to the creative person (me!). So we ended up creating a beautiful, heart-warming, full-color brochure of a wonderful young man. It cost a fortune to print, and thus made the cost of the mailing very high. In the end, that mailing was a great addition to my creative portfolio, but it did not bring in enough orders or inquiries for the insurance company to pay for producing so expensive a mailing package. Essentially, the first marketing guideline, *cost-effectiveness*, was violated.

I could cite many more examples of programs, services, and resources that were not successfully marketed because one of the three guidelines of marketing—cost-effectiveness, finding the right people, and timing—were not carefully considered. All three are vital.

Content is Just the Beginning

Marketing is everywhere. My first boss had a poster in his office that had a photo of a young, well-dressed business man. It said something like this: "Hate advertising? So does this man— who got up this morning, brushed his teeth with his favorite advertised brand of toothpaste, took a shower using his preferred advertised brand of soap, shaved using an aftershave he discovered after viewing a television commercial, ate a bowl of his favorite advertised cereal, got into the car he found through an advertisement on the radio, and headed off to the job he found through a local newspaper advertisement."

This poster reminds me that, like it or not, advertising and marketing are all around us. We cannot escape it. And it is not just in the commercial sense. The e-mails we get at work about professional development opportunities, the newsletters we get at home from our healthcare provider, and the Web site we consult on the Internet to help us write a paper are forms of promotion and advertising. Even the way we present ourselves—what we wear, how we speak, and how we carry ourselves—are a type of marketing.

Why does marketing matter? As career development experts, why should we be concerned about planning and marketing? Isn't the quality of the content of what we deliver all that really matters? It's not uncommon to hear comments like this, particularly from people in education or counseling. After all, they are in the business of teaching, training, and counseling—not selling. Yet, the reality is that marketing does make a difference—a *big* difference.

Without adequate or informed marketing, the applicability of content to the audience, the method of delivery, the format of the program or service, the price or timing of services, and dozens of other variables can go wrong. Sound marketing includes *planning* what you will offer, *implementing* the steps to create and deliver it, and *informing others* about it. Each of these plays an important role in your career development program, and each is critical.

Nowhere is the importance of a comprehensive approach to marketing more evident than in the design of a career development training program. An overlooked detail or a careless error in the planning or implementation of an event can lead to a complete failure. Below are some of the factors to consider. Although not comprehensive, this list will give you an idea of the decisions and details you need to consider when you plan the development of a product or program. The same attention to detail and thoughtful planning shown here applies to any undertaking that includes marketing (e.g., delivering career counseling services, writing a brochure or book, developing a class or presentation). From start to finish, attention to detail and remembering the big picture help ensure a positive result. Some of the factors to consider in planning and marketing any event include:

When. What else is going on at the same time? Are there competing activities or other events that may cause conflicts for people who want to participate? Have you considered when other local or industry events are occurring? Is there anything happening in your community, the industry, or the broader world (e.g., an election, a major sporting event, a holiday weekend) that might influence attendance?

Where. What meeting spaces are available on your preferred dates and times? Is there a cost for using the space, and if so, is it in your budget? Is convenient parking available? If your audience uses public transportation, is it accessible to your potential site?

Timing. Is one season or time of year better suited for the needs of your audience? What about time of the day or week? For example, if your intended audience is executives considering early retirement, avoid planning your event during a regular 9–5 workday when they will be unable to attend due to work obligations.

How to tell others (i.e., how to promote and advertise it). Will you send e-mails, create a flyer, or send a mailing? Whatever method is chosen, check all the details for accuracy. Sending out a flyer with a typo in the street address of the site could prove disastrous for people unfamiliar with the location. Forgetting to include a phone number, e-mail, or Web site address will prevent people from contacting you with questions or to register.

Budgeting and expenses. How much can you afford to pay for advertising, audiovisual equipment, and materials? Will you need to pay a speaker or cover travel or other related expenses? Plan for every single expenditure you will incur so that you don't end up losing money on an event that was intended to generate revenue.

Logistics. Consider every detail including technology, hospitality, seating, and a myriad of other concerns to keep a small item from ruining the entire event or program. For example, consider what would happen if your attendees arrive at the workshop site on the planned day to find that the door is locked and no one has a key to get in the building. Small details are as important to an event's success as the time spent preparing the presentation.

What's in a Name: Other Marketing Terms

There are a number of different terms that are often used interchangeably with the words *marketing* and *promotion. Advertising* is one of the terms we hear often. In general, advertising brings a product or service to the attention of potential customers (or clients or students). We see and hear advertising around us every day. Some examples are television commercials, computer pop-ups, radio spots, billboards, brochures, e-mails, posters, and Web sites. *Promotion* keeps a product or service in the customer's mind and stimulates demand. Promotion generally refers to ongoing activity rather than a one-time effort. For example, press coverage and publicity are examples of *promotion,* the umbrella term that refers to any activity designed to disseminate information and attract attention. They can be used over time to create a certain perception or image in the mind of the intended audience.

Public relations refers to ongoing activities that ensure a strong public image. Public relations includes work through the media, such as newspaper, television, radio, and magazine coverage. In public relations efforts, you (and your organization) are in control, deciding when and where to inform others. One way to clarify the meaning of public relations is to think about a company that calls a press conference to address safety or another concern. The company is in charge of the press conference, and the company decides what will be stated. In *publicity,* on the other hand, the media is in control, deciding which stories to run and how to tell them. Think about what stories were on the front page of your newspaper last night or at the top of the news broadcast and you will see how publicity is controlled by a person in power who decides what is important and how to portray that to the general audience. *Sales* is also a part of marketing and usually includes activities such as finding people who will be interested in your offering (cultivating leads), clearly explaining what your product or service is and how it could assist them (conveying features, advantages, and benefits), and following through to get attendees or complete the purchase (closing the sale). *Customer service* is often the final step in the marketing effort and refers to the delivery of products or services and follow-up with the customer or client.

The Marketing Mix

There are many different components of marketing. Promotional activities are the part we may think of first when we discuss marketing, but there are other considerations in overall marketing too, such as positioning, pricing, strategy, and assessment. One reason for developing a complete marketing plan is so that you can pay attention to the many variables that will play a role in the success of your marketing and not overlook any critical considerations. All the pieces of your marketing mix are interconnected and must be considered in relationship to the others. For example, positioning will affect promotions, and pricing will connect with program planning. Each component must be considered in connection with the whole.

Successful marketing, including the marketing of career development services and programs, can include just one, all, or, as in most cases, a combination of several activities and elements. It really doesn't matter what terms you use when talking about your marketing and promotional efforts, but it does help to know about the options available for you to choose from. Marketing is similar to a puzzle where many different pieces must fit together in order to make the whole thing come together to function most effectively. The wide range of activities and components that help marketers meet the needs of their customers include, but are not limited to:

- mailings,
- e-mails,
- lists,
- flyers,
- posters,
- research,
- brochures,
- Web sites,
- pricing,
- positioning,
- branding,

- strategizing,
- customer feedback,
- word of mouth,
- publicity, and
- press releases.

The diagram in Appendix A illustrates how the marketing strategy is central to all the other components of your marketing mix. Setting a strategy and plan is a matter that should influence all marketing activities and decisions as you move along in your marketing continuum.

Choosing a Marketing Vehicle

Since the growth of the Internet, there is a wider variety of marketing options available. Which types of marketing vehicles you use will depend upon your goals, resources, budget, and expertise. To begin, think about your marketing goals, including who you are trying to reach. Consider how much money, time, and assistance you have available to reach out to your audience. For instance, if you know your audience will read a brochure, how much money do you have to print a brochure? Will you have to do the writing and the design, or is there someone else who will supply expertise in that area? How will you get that brochure out to your audience? Will you need to mail it? If so, do you have the budget for postage? If you are distributing brochures, will you need to do this yourself or are there others you can network with to help get the brochures circulated? These questions will help you determine which marketing vehicle(s) to use:

- Objective: What am I trying to do?
- What is the most appropriate method to achieve this?
- What is the cost of using this method?
- Will this reach the right people?
- Is there a less costly or free alternative (especially for smaller organizations or individuals)?

No matter which channels you decide to use for your promotions, you'll need to consider from the beginning whether you have the necessary resources to use that channel effectively. Below are some of the methods that are available to get your message out to potential customers.

Different Marketing Methods Suit Varying Needs

Mailings are materials, usually in the form of a letter

and envelope with possible additional pieces such as a brochure, that are mailed to the *prospect,* or intended customer. Postcards and self-mailers are also mailings. In the *direct response* industry, a trackable reply resulting from the marketing activity, in this case the mailing, is integral to the marketing materials. True direct response activities include not just mailings, but also telemarketing (phone call) activity, advertisements, e-mails, and any other marketing activity where the number of responses can be traced directly to the marketing effort.

Since most career development practitioners will not have the resources to directly track responses to their efforts, it is a good idea to have some means of determining if your marketing efforts are working. In many cases, that will simply be watching how many calls, orders, or registrations come in after conducting your promotional campaign. One way to do this is to ask people how they found out about you. Mailings are generally expensive because postage must be added in addition to the cost of printing and development of the materials. If you have a way to disseminate materials without using postage (such as stuffing materials into the mailboxes of staff, students, or educators) you will be able to save on postage costs. A key factor to successful mailings is making sure that a good customer or prospective customer list is used so that you are reaching out, or *targeting,* the correct audience.

This may be a good spot to briefly discuss the compilation of a *prospect list.* A prospect list contains contact information of individuals you think may be interested in your services or programs. This list usually includes mailing addresses, e-mail addresses, or both. Large companies, of course, have sophisticated databases and complete departments that handle this important marketing function. But even the private practice career counselor should be constantly updating and maintaining a prospect file, as well as a customer file. A resourceful marketer makes prospects a priority at all times and makes a point of adding the names and contact information of every possible client or buyer to their list on a regular basis. It is easy to start your own prospect list using a simple Excel file or Access database. Whatever method you choose, be constantly on the lookout for possible customers, and you will grow your prospect database over time. Yes, it takes time to compile these lists, but doing so is important to the success of your marketing endeavors. More information about lists compilation and selection will be included later in this monograph.

Telemarketing consists of a telephone call to the prospect. We all have had the personal experience of being interrupted at dinnertime with a telemarketing call. But not all telemarketing needs to be annoying. Telemarketing can be used to achieve positive results with a highly targeted group of potential or past customers with whom you have a close tie. Usually telemarketing is considered a costly way to market. However, if your service is personalized, then telemarketing may be a viable route and can be as simple as making personal phone calls to referrals or past customers. Colleges and universities have caught on to this "personal phone call" strategy and are having current students make phone calls to alumni to ask for financial support. Nonprofit organizations, such as churches, use this method when they have your neighbor call you to ask for financial support. This general strategy of approaching someone you know, also known as *friend-to-friend* or *referral* marketing, can be used with positive results in many different marketing applications. It may be worthwhile to consider telemarketing for follow-up and customer service after an event, particularly if your audience is small.

Newsletters sent to prospects and/or customers allow you to keep in touch with them on a regular basis. The key to success with this method is including new or interesting information relevant to the audience, and secondarily adding information about your latest offer. Newsletters allow you to build a relationship with your customer. This relationship has been proven to be the most effective way to reach an audience and create customer loyalty. Electronic newsletters are less costly than printed newsletters, but your method will depend upon the reading habits of your audience and on your budget. Similar to regular newsletters, *blogs, e-seminars,* or *podcasts* can be used as a regular means of staying in touch with your customers. These methods will be discussed in more detail later in the Electronic Marketing section.

Press releases are often a forgotten means of getting the word out, but they shouldn't be. It costs nothing to write a press release, and it earns you free publicity. Draw up a list of interested media contacts and send out information via e-mail. If they run the release, great! If not, you haven't lost anything but the time it took you to write it. Anyone can write a press release. If you are not sure if you can, then search online for some material that will show you how. I am often amazed at the number of people who don't take advantage of this simple way to promote their career development offerings. It really is free publicity. In

Appendix B, I have included a few tips on writing press releases that can help you get started or, if you are already writing press releases, can help increase the chances that your news releases will be placed in the media.

Presentations and meetings provide opportunities to speak publicly and to network with others. It is a good idea to always take along brochures or flyers if you attend meetings, conferences, or other events where possible contacts may be present. When giving presentations, briefly mention what you and your organization or department have planned for the future. Perhaps most importantly, use the contacts you make at these gatherings to follow up with afterwards. It is a great idea to send a friendly e-mail after such a meeting to stay in touch and to include information "just in case you or someone you know may be interested."

Bulletin board notices, a low-tech way to promote your services, are especially appropriate if you work with students and educators. At schools and colleges, staff and students view bulletin boards on a regular basis. Businesses and companies, too, often have bulletin boards that personnel regularly skim while waiting for the elevator or getting a drink at the water fountain. Putting up a flyer or a brochure is inexpensive advertising that will let you reach your target audience where they are located.

Flyers and brochures are a method often used to promote products and services when you have a limited budget and resources. For these materials, you will need someone who can write and design effective materials. You will also incur printing costs. Consider using copiers in place of actual printers for smaller runs of printed items. Color copiers can often be used as an inexpensive way to create attractive brochures and flyers without the cost of print shop services.

Technology Provides New Options for Marketers

E-mails can take the place of direct mailing at a fraction of the cost. It is relatively easy to send an e-mail out to potential or current customers. However, there also are challenges when using e-mail, and these challenges are increasing every day. More and more e-mails are being blocked as they come into a group or individual's mail system by increasingly sophisticated filters. If you use e-mails, you will need to take reasonable steps to keep your message from being blocked by filters and marked as spam. E-mails are

most appropriate when you want to communicate quickly and incur no expenses. An e-mail "blast" refers to the process of sending out e-mails to a large group of individuals at once.

Web sites can be used to promote your services and products to individuals who are likely to already know you, or who may be searching for similar services by keyword. The creation of a Web site takes a large amount of expertise and resources compared to many other methods of promotion. Not only will you need a host for your Web page as well as appropriate software, but you will also need a knowledgeable person who can create, design, and maintain the site. It is becoming easier for non-technical people to create their own Web sites with today's new Web design software programs, but keep in mind that you also need to be able to maintain your Web site if you choose to use this method of promotion. Web sites can go a long way toward contributing to your "branding," which will be discussed later in this monograph. For that reason, they can be an important part of an overall marketing strategy for individuals and companies who choose to invest in them.

Online listings, such as *eCalendars* (which are calendars of events that can be found on some association or group Web sites) are a great way to get some free advertising. Think about the associations and groups that have members who may be interested in what you have to offer. Then e-mail or call contacts from those groups to see if they'd be willing to post information about your event or programs online. It costs nothing to ask and can help you expand your reach if the organization agrees to post your information. You might also consider asking the group if it will send your message by e-mail to its members, or post information on its electronic mailing list, blog, or newsletter.

Links to other Web sites are another easy and inexpensive way to promote if you have your own Web site. Ask colleagues and professional contacts if they will provide a link to your Web page from their Web site. It is a cost-free way to help you reach the right kind of individual, essentially functioning as electronic "word of mouth."

Electronic mailing lists are groups of people who have signed up to receive and post information on a chosen topic of interest. Members of an electronic mailing list receive regular e-mails from other members. There are electronic mailing lists for nearly all industries and interests. Rules vary for each electronic mailing list so be sure you have permission before posting promotional material. Electronic mailing lists are a good way to reach a group of people who have shown an interest in similar topics.

Blogs have now found their way into every industry and field. Blogs, considered personal online journals when they first began, are rapidly replacing newsletters for keeping individuals up to date on the latest resources and news. Creating a quality, informative blog can help you create a more personal link with your audience. It is probably not the best way to reach prospects, unless you are a well-known expert who people may be searching for online. Similar to blogs are *online chat groups* and discussion groups, where you can informally discuss your programs and make contacts with others interested in similar topics.

Networking Web sites, such as MySpace and Facebook, are growing in popularity, especially with younger people. These sites permit users to create their own Web pages that may include text, music, and photos. Viewers can see the pages and post responses, creating a "network". New sites are being created on a regular basis, some focusing on a particular topic or interest. Although they are not commonly used for marketing purposes today, networking sites may become a viable marketing tool in the future as they continue to expand in number and variety.

Webinars, or *e-seminars,* are being used more and more frequently to reach customers and potential customers. These are events that are scheduled online that the audience views either from their own personal computer or in a group setting via satellite. Sometimes these "online seminars" are used to deliver training, such as a workshop on interviewing. Other times, the webinar or e-seminar serves as a promotional tool in much the same way as a well-written, content-laden newsletter. That is, it provides information that the audience wants and serves the purpose of helping to build a longer term relationship with the customer. The growing use of these electronic seminars or workshops also aids in building the brand of the host group or individual, a concept that will be discussed later in this monograph.

Podcasts are digital recordings of audio programs that are made available for downloading to an iPod or similar audio player through the Internet. Podcasts are generally used for presentations or programs and can include a mix of music and voice. However, podcasts can be used as a promotional tool if the subject matter lends itself to related content and mention of your offerings can be included. Similar to a radio program, speakers and guests on podcasts can speak to the audience to build loyalty, interest, and credibility for you and your organization.

The pyramid below illustrates the time, cost, and expertise required to use some of the most common types of promotions. Those at the top require the least investment of time, money, and expertise, starting with writing a press release. Those at the bottom require the greatest investment, such as creating and maintaining a Web site or producing a webinar.

Diagram A. Pyramid of Common Marketing Methods

Requires least amount of time, money, or expertise

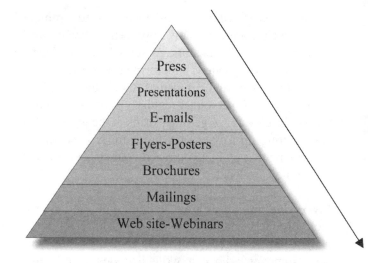

Requires greatest amount of time, money, or expertise

Clearly, the marketing methods near the top of the pyramid are those that can be most easily used by the sole practitioner or someone who has limited resources and a low promotional budget. In addition to press releases, word of mouth, mention at presentations, sending e-mails, and similar low-tech options require no additional expenses. Moving down the pyramid are methods that require some design knowledge and print or copying elements—such as creating brochures, flyers, or posters. Mailings are even more costly because of the additional cost of postage and the complexities of choosing and producing mailing lists. Finally, high-tech options such as Web sites, e-seminars, webcasts, and similar new methods require staff with knowledge and expertise, as well as monetary investment or access to new technologies.

Chapter 2
Developing Your Marketing Plan

Given time constraints and deadlines, practitioners may be tempted to jump directly into writing their brochure or flyer as the first step in their marketing. However, several issues must first be addressed and incorporated into a marketing plan if one wants to conduct marketing and promotional campaigns that achieve his or her goals.

In this section, we will explore some of the primary elements that make up any well-planned marketing campaign (no matter how large or small), including a description of how each of these elements contributes to the success of the program as a whole. While a variety of planning models are available, I suggest that every practitioner start with a simple five-step model. For large corporations or those working with complex campaigns, the marketing plan could encompass 100 pages. For many career development practitioners, addressing the items in this simple five-part process will be enough to launch a well thought-out campaign for the development and promotion of their programs and services.

The model I recommend includes five elements:

1. Market research
2. Program design
3. Marketing strategy
4. Promotional activities
5. Customer service and feedback

The components of each of these elements is explored below, with ideas for how each can be incorporated or adapted to fit specific uses.

1. Market Research

Market research is one of the most important activities for successful marketing, yet one that is often overlooked. Many failed marketing efforts are due to not doing the homework required before launching out. Before you begin planning your next program or service, take the time to conduct some research. This will allow you to start your planning from an informed state. Addressing market research considerations from the beginning will result in a better product or program. The program or product will then be planned to fit the needs of your audience and to produce a satisfactory outcome. This research begins with a study of your audience.

Audience

I cannot overstate the importance of knowing who you are trying to reach. The makeup of your audience—and the habits and mindsets of individuals in your audience—forms the basis of any sound marketing and promotional effort. Different types of people have varying needs and ways of responding to the world around them. The savvy marketer will want to know what those needs are and to explore the best ways to meet them. Consider the differences between a chronically unemployed 42-year-old male veteran with a GED and a history of mental illness and a 21-year-old middle-class female recently graduated from college with honors and a B.A. in history. Not only are the employment needs and life situations of these individuals different, but the ways that you would plan, market, and promote your services to each also vary. Some of the differences between these people may include knowledge of available resources, ability to self-start and self-motivate, access to transportation, ability to pay for services, level of necessary outside interventions, and level of computer literacy. Additionally, these two individuals will respond differently to your marketing and promotional efforts. The avenues that you use in reaching out to them may be quite different. The veteran may need to be approached with flyers mailed to him or posters at the community job or veteran's center, while the recent graduate may be reached through e-mails, a Web site, or brochures mailed or displayed in the college placement office.

While having knowledge about your customer may seem obvious, I recommend that you delve further into this area and perform a written exercise detailing who makes up your audience. You may be surprised at what you discover when you take the time to consciously expand your understanding of your audience. Putting this down in writing and taking the time to consider the needs and abilities of your audience before planning can save you time and money. When working with a team, this helps everyone share their understanding of who they are trying to reach and can catalyze a discussion of how best to reach them. More information on getting to know your audience is included in the section on Painting a Customer Profile.

Competition

The next element in informed market research is studying the competition. Whether you are planning a workshop or seminar, setting up advising hours, or doing any other outreach, it is essential that you know who you are competing against. If you plan to put on a series of workshops on job seeking and someone in your area is doing the same thing, it is important that you know that before you start expending time, money, and resources. Find out what others are doing, take a look at their focus, examine how much they are charging, and investigate how your offer is different or similar. Perhaps you will determine that there is enough interest in your area to support two successful workshop series on a topic. However, your research could also lead you to change the focus of your workshop material, or you might price it differently. On the other hand, you might choose not to move ahead after taking the competition fully into consideration.

History

Here is where you will need to look at the history of your organization's offerings. Are there programs and services that have been offered in the past? What was successful and what was not? How can you build on things that worked and learn from the things that didn't? Take a look at past reports, surveys, and evaluations, and consider how you can apply that information. Talk to past customers, your staff, and others who can tell you what has worked and why. You can then use historical information to strengthen your program and service design, delivery, and marketability. It is a good idea to start a file that documents the offerings made and outcomes achieved through your efforts or those of your organization. This file can be expanded as your experience in your marketplace grows. It can save you time to have all this information in one place and readily accessible when you consider launching a new program or marketing endeavor.

2. Program Design

In this portion of your planning, you state what you are trying to achieve (your goals) and how you are going to achieve those goals (your strategies). The temptation at this stage is to skip this step, assuming that you already know them or that you don't have the time. But, as with your audience profile, it is useful to put down in writing what you are trying to achieve and the simple ideas of how you are going to get there. This is especially true if you are working with a team. Putting these notions on paper can help the group discover and address discrepancies early in the process, and avoid problems later when misunderstandings may surface or when the goal is obscured by immediate concerns. With a written plan, everyone can begin working with the same shared understanding, goals, and intentions.

To begin, clarify what program or service you plan to deliver (e.g., workshop, career counseling sessions, assessments). Just as in the other planning stages, follow basic marketing tenets (discussed in detail in Chapter 3). This will enable you to plan programs and services that will meet the needs of your intended audience. Your marketing strategy and the marketing research you have done will be used to design a program that fits your target market.

A number of key marketing issues should be addressed in this phase of planning. Like many of the marketing concepts discussed in this monograph, these matters are integrated with others throughout the planning, promotion, and implementation processes.

1. Explain what you are offering or proposing. Outline exactly what you are going to deliver.
2. Determine when, where, and how. Think about the feasibility of various options using the customer information you have developed.
3. Estimate the costs. A simple Excel spreadsheet can track estimated expenses,
4. Set your price. This will be determined by how much income you need, while considering competitors' offerings and what the market will bear.
5. Plan the curriculum, create the agenda, etc. List the specifics of the program/service you are developing.
6. Pay attention to details and logistics. They can make or break a program.

3. Marketing Strategy/Plan

While there are dozens of types of marketing plans available, from short and sweet to lengthy and complex, I recommend that career development practitioners start with a simple model and add on to it as needed. At a minimum, a sound marketing strategy should address the following points:

- Objective: What you want to achieve
- Who: Definition of your market
- Methods: How you will do this
- Timing: When you will do this
- Resources: What you need to make this happen
- Costs: Estimated expenses and income
- Promotions: What you will do and when
- Outcome: How will you measure achievement or success

A blank template of this planning model is included in Appendix C. This template can be copied and used for individuals or for groups of practitioners who are working together to develop programs and services. For complicated projects or full campaigns, the model will serve as a simple cover sheet of items to be discussed. More pages and details will need to be added. But for many career practitioners, this simple model is enough to help achieve focus and address key marketing considerations that will affect planning of a simple project or offering.

Below is an example of how this template can be used in its simplest form for a practitioner planning a series of workshops. Even at this level, having this plan completed and written out will help provide focus and direction in the planning process. It will also provide a way to check that the most important aspects of the planning process have been addressed.

Table 1. Sample of a Basic Marketing Plan

OBJECTIVE: What do I want to achieve?	*My objective is to assist people in career transitions through training that is focused on how to explore new job or career opportunities.*
WHO: Define my audience	*For professionals (in or out of work) in the Madison area who are considering a career change either out of necessity (job loss) or desire (wanting a change).*
METHODS: How will I achieve this?	*I will conduct two 2-hour workshops on this topic. I will also provide one-on-one counseling as requested by individuals who attend the workshops.*
WHEN: What is the timeframe or day/time?	*The workshops will be held on two consecutive Wednesday evenings in October, from 7:00 to 9:00 pm. The counseling will be by appointment only during late afternoons and evenings during the months of October (after classes begin) through November.*
REQUIRED RESOURCES: What people/tools or other is needed to accomplish this?	*• Reserve a meeting room in the public library* *• Two laptops with Internet connections* *• Instructional materials* *• Photocopies of all handouts* *• Instructor for two evenings (myself)* *• Office for counseling appointments*
ESTIMATED COSTS: Attach a budget sheet showing cost/income projections	*Attach a simple Excel worksheet showing expenses and income (see sample in Appendix D.)*
PROMOTIONS: How will I let my audience know?	*August: Create flyer and post on job boards. Send e-mails to appropriate lists. Place notices on e-calendars and electronic mailing lists.* *September: Distribute flyers to local job or career counselors and groups. Write cover letter and send to local HR reps and unemployment agencies. Create space ad for job center and other newsletters.* *October: Send additional and follow-up e-mails. Call personal contacts at agencies, etc.*
MEASURE OF ACHIEVEMENT/OUTCOMES: How will I tell if I was successful?	*Will create an evaluation form and will collect it on the last day of class for feedback. Need to at least break even financially to be considered successful.*

Whether you choose to use this model or another for planning, it is important that your plan be written down. My personal experience (in addition to what I have heard from other careers practitioners) has taught me that if it is not written down at the beginning, it is easy to make mistakes as your project takes shape. The first potential mistake is that you can lose the "big picture" and become so bogged down in the details that you forget what you are trying to achieve. The second is the danger that important details will be overlooked, leading to problems or even failure of the program. By writing this plan at the beginning, everyone has something to consult throughout the process and a reference to use when questions come up.

4. Promotional Activities

Marketing and promotional activities are an essential ingredient of a well-designed and executed service or program. Many people consider the planning and execution of promotional activities to be the "fun" part of marketing. Others, who may have entered this area without any background or experience, find it to be the most challenging part. Promotions matter because, no matter how outstanding your service or product, if no one knows about it, or if no one is convinced of its value, then all your planning and hard work will not pay off.

There are many lessons about promotional and advertising activities that can be gleaned from the field of consumer marketing. Among these are some fundamental concepts and practices that can be applied to any kind of marketing and promotional effort. At the same time, some of the advertising and promotional practices we see every day will not be transferable to career development–related marketing. Much of the rest of this monograph will provide information that can be used to decide what promotional activities best fit your situation, and how to make those promotional activities most effective. The goal of providing this information is to give you general guidelines about what constitutes effective marketing practice, regardless of what you are selling or promoting. By taking these general principles and applying them to your specific situation, you will be able to strengthen the promotional aspect of your program, and ensure that it becomes an integral part of your comprehensive planning and program implementation.

When completing your marketing strategy/plan, you should write down specifically which means of marketing and promotional methods you plan to use. This could include brochures, mailings, e-mails, or any other of the methods to be discussed later. It is a good idea to include deadlines or target dates for developing and disseminating your marketing and promotions. It takes time to develop promotional materi-als, and you need to be sure that sufficient time is included so that you reach out to your intended audience at the appropriate time.

5. Customer Service and Feedback

Getting feedback from your customers is the final component of any marketing plan. Useful information can be obtained through a paper or electronic survey, telemarketing phone calls, or word of mouth. Finding out what worked and what didn't work will help you improve on your future efforts, and give you valuable information that can tell you what your audience needs, wants, and likes. The opinions of your customers can be obtained continuously throughout the process, or it can be a one-time response. The information obtained in this step, once collected and analyzed, becomes a part of your market research when you begin your next marketing strategy.

Don't forget to ask clients and customers why they hired you or purchased your materials. Or send out a survey to past or potential customers to find out what you are doing right and what can be improved. One caution about surveys: If you ask for feedback, you will most likely hear about the extremes at both ends. You will receive feedback from those who *love* your offerings and those who *hate* them. When assessing customer feedback, look for trends in responses and for new opportunities that you may not have considered.

Reaching the customer service and feedback stage indicates that you have gone full circle in your critical planning. That is because the information you gain in this fifth step feeds back into the first step of the process—market research. The feedback you get from customers will be added to the market research you did at the beginning and be carefully considered as you move on to your next endeavor. In this way, this five-step marketing plan is a continuous process. Each step feeds into the following step. So, although the process is linear in some ways, it is also circular and continuous.

Diagram B. Relationship of the Components of a Marketing Plan

Chapter 3
How to Create Promotions

Now we will examine the marketing function most often connected with the term "marketing," that is, creating promotional materials that attract customers and clients. There is no secret to creating effective print and electronic promotional materials, but there are ideas, tips, and principles that will lead to stronger, more effective campaigns and activities. This section will explain some underlying concepts of marketing and advertising, and present practical techniques and principles to enhance your promotion of careers-related programs and services. These principles are based upon proven results of marketing tests and will hold true for any type of marketing.

Principle 1: Start with Your Customer

The absolute most important part of marketing is meeting the needs of the customer. I cannot overstate the importance of this principle. Everything else pales in comparison to this concept, and nothing else matters if you get this wrong. If you are not in touch with the wants and needs of your potential audience(s), then no matter what else you do, your efforts will not be successful. Marketing requires you to step out of your own shoes and into the shoes of your audience. Who is your audience and what services will meet its needs? For those who deliver career development services, this step requires a reversal of the way we usually approach the development and delivery of services.

While sitting in strategic planning meetings, I've observed something about planning that occurs in organizations large, small, and in between. People's first tendency is to start program planning by focusing on what *we have to offer,* not what *the customer needs* or desires. We must learn to step out of the role of the practitioner and into the role of the audience so that we can see things from the customer's perspective. This helps in developing and delivering services geared to the audience's needs, not geared to our own needs or to those of our organization.

Painting a Customer Profile

Creating a profile of your audience is a good way to get in touch with the needs of your customers. The Paint a Customer Profile worksheet in Appendix E is an exercise that can help you define your audience and begin to understand its needs. I recommend that you complete this exercise at the beginning of your planning. This will help you better understand your customer. The more you know about your audience, the better able you will be to design services and products that are appropriate and relevant. This is so critical that absolutely no marketing should be done before a customer profile is completed. Although you probably already know some things about your customer, doing this exercise will make you think more deeply about your audience's needs, wants, lifestyle, and mindset. Your customer knowledge plays a part in every step of the marketing process, from program design to promotional activities to customer feedback.

Demographics: *Who* is your audience?

The Paint a Customer Profile worksheet is designed to assist you in considering two important parts of defining your audience. The first of these is audience *demographics*. These include the external factors that define your audience's lifestyle and external characteristics. In this section, you pinpoint such variables as the customer's age, ethnicity, income level, gender, educational level, place of residence (urban, rural, suburban), and additional factors that define the lifestyle of your customer. Identifying these characteristics will assist you in multiple ways by providing information that can be used to market appropriately for your particular audience.

For example, let's take the case of a student advisor who works in a job center at a large university. The typical customers for this practitioner may meet this profile:

- age 18–22,
- low income (college students generally do not have much money of their own),
- ½ male and ½ female,
- usually live on campus or near campus, from a mix of urban, rural, and suburban communities,
- graduated in the upper 35% of their high school class,

- 25% work while attending school, and most do not have access to a car but can ride public transportation.

When completing your customer profile, include any factors that you can define. If you have customers of varying types, you could do one profile for each of your demographic groups. This will help ensure that you design services and programs to meet the needs of each type of customer and may influence your decisions about what to offer. For example, if your audience is made up of people who are unemployed as well as people who are employed 9–5 on weekdays, you may decide to design two separate workshop series, one held during the workday and one held in the evenings.

There are other factors to consider in your profile as well. Do your customers have childcare issues? Transportation or parking needs? What hours are they generally available and are they able to pay for services? Do they have computer skills and access to computers? Think about where they are likely to get information about your organization and your services. Are they members of certain associations or organizations? Do they have access to specific bulletin boards or Web sites? Are they a group that would regularly check e-mails? Using demographics in this way can help you determine the best means of outreach for your audience.

Psychographics: How do they *think and respond?*

Identifying *psychographics,* the second portion of completing a customer profile, is more challenging. Yet defining your customers' psychographics can provide a terrific advantage in marketing. Psychographics refers to the psychology behind your typical customer. Given the information you have from the customer demographics, psychographics sheds light on how customers may think about or react to specific topics, ideas, or words. You can use this knowledge to design offerings and write promotions in ways that will attract your targeted audience and elicit positive reactions.

Marketing is a way of managing your program so that each critical decision is made with full knowledge of the impact it will have on the customer. Using the audience defined above as an example (18–22 year old students at a large university), what can we learn from the demographic profile that will indicate how to successfully market to this group? First, given their young age, we can make some assumptions about their use of technology. They are probably connected to the Internet on a daily basis. Therefore, it would be appropriate to use electronic means of communicating with them. E-mails and Web sites could be considered, as well as possible electronic delivery formats like Webinars (sometimes called e-seminars) or podcasts. Since students are located on or near campus, they may have contact with bulletin boards in campus buildings, so that may be another method of promotion that would be useful. There may be a number of other promotional methods that are appropriate for use with this group and considering the demographics of the group can help illuminate them.

We can make additional deductions that will assist in designing programs and promoting them specifically to this group. For example, it would be useful to think about what matters to people in this group. What is important to 18–22 year-old college students and how can we use that to draw them to our services? (For example, you might provide free pizza at a meeting because students come to events with free food.) Creating this kind of psychographic profile requires that the practitioner be in tune with the audience and be willing to think through how the profile may affect members' thinking and decision making. If you have worked with the audience long enough, you may know this information instinctively. If not, then gathering this information can be done in a number of ways, including surveys, focus groups, informal conversations, or through contacting people who interact directly with your intended audience (such as student advisors, instructors, or campus employers, in this case). Some other ways to learn more about your audience include reading trade and popular magazines, viewing Web sites and reading blogs, joining related electronic mailing lists, attending organizational or association meetings, and reading about the demographics of your group. There are many Web sites that can be found with a search engine that will inform you about the mindset of your audience, particularly related to their generation.

Another example of how to use psychographics in marketing is to explore the language and words that are most appealing or appropriate for your intended customers. If your audience is comprised of low-income single mothers, you would not use the same approach or terminology as you would with a group made up of well-paid executives who have recently been laid off from corporate positions. You must consider the motivation, desires, and needs of the group and be sure to address those in your offerings. Again, using the college student example, this means that marketing materials would use language that is familiar to this age group and to their educational level.

Principle 2: Know Your "Niche"

There is a term in marketing and advertising called the *unique selling proposition* or USP. It refers to the unique factor or factors that make what you deliver distinct and different from all the others. This *niche* should be emphasized in your marketing and promotional materials and strategy. It is the characteristic or feature that you want to emphasize to your customers. Remember that people are bombarded with information every day. Your advertising should make it immediately clear why your particular product or service is different, and why it is the one that your prospect should consider.

Positioning

Closely related to knowing your niche is the concept of *positioning*. This is marketing that emphasizes how you want to be perceived in the customer's mind or what place you want to occupy there. As with the USP or niche, this strategy focuses on what sets your offering apart from the rest. To create your niche or USP, spend some time thinking about what is unique about you or what you offer and then find a way to communicate that. If you offer career counseling, what do you have to offer that is different from what your clients can get somewhere else? If you have a workbook on job hunting, why would someone pick yours to read over the dozens of others available? The unique selling proposition should answer the customer's question: Why should I choose this one over all the others? Much of consumer advertising uses a USP, and it is just as appropriate and necessary for marketing career development products and services. There are many ways to address the issue of what makes you and your service different. Summarizing it into one phrase will force you to state your USP succinctly and clearly. Here are a few examples of USPs for career development offerings:

- The conference for practitioners
- Your one stop for career training and development
- Personalized counseling for Manitowoc job seekers

Target Marketing

Another concept related to niche and positioning in the world of marketing is *target marketing*. Target marketing is just what it sounds like—it is creating promotions and advertising that is aimed at or *targeted* for a specific group of people. Similar to niche marketing, positioning, and unique selling proposition, target marketing is based on common sense. If you "target" or aim for the correct group of people, your marketing efforts will "hit the target" and be successful. Likewise, if you have wonderful promotional material, but send it to the wrong target, or people, it will miss the mark and be unsuccessful.

A complete industry has grown up around target marketing, along with the development and refinement of customer and prospect databases. By tracking specific characteristics of individuals, database companies can now provide lists of individuals who meet the characteristics of a marketer's ideal audience. This essentially narrows down the audience, so that marketing materials can be sent to a smaller group of people who most closely fit the intended audience. Mailing to a smaller, but more closely matched, group of individuals will always save costs because fewer materials need to be printed and distributed.

Here is an example of target marketing in the area of education marketing. Let's say I want to mail a flyer about a course for career development to counselors in a school setting. Working with a mailing list company that specializes in education, I can select increasingly narrow parameters of available characteristics, or *selections,* to produce a list of individuals who most closely match those I want to mail.

First I select by job title, choosing individuals with the title of "counselor" or "guidance counselor." Next, I select those titles for certain educational levels, such as high school and middle school only. Next I narrow that down further by targeting individuals with these job titles at these levels that are in public schools. To further narrow down the list, I may choose certain zip codes only, so that I only reach out to individuals meeting these criteria who are in Midwest states only. The list of items to be selected varies with the sophistication of the database used. But variables such as school spending limits, Title I status, neighborhood wealth indicators, and many others can be selected.

Although most of us will not do large enough or sophisticated enough mailings to employ this level of selection, there is a general principle of marketing here that should be employed in all marketing and promotional efforts. It is that the more closely you match (or target) your intended audience with your current audience, the more successful and cost-effective your marketing efforts will be.

The diagram below indicates how this principle is applied when deciding to whom to distribute promotional and advertising material for a workshop on the subject of writing resumes. The closer the relationship or link you have with your targeted audience, the higher the response you will obtain. When you are deciding how to spend your budget for marketing and promotional activities and how to best reach the people most likely to respond, start with those who have some previous contact with you (called *past buyers* in the marketing field), move on to those who have some link or knowledge of your organization (such as *inquiries*), then move on to people who have done business with a similar organization (such as a competitor's list). Finally, approach the true *prospects*, i.e., those individuals who have a possible interest, but no proven experience, link, or purchasing history.

Diagram C. Proximity of List Types to Current Clients

Closeness to center indicates likelihood of positive promotional results

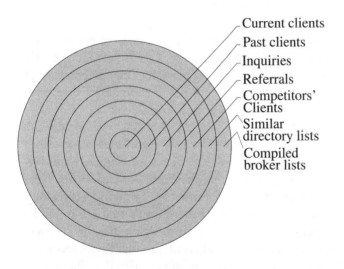

Current clients
Past clients
Inquiries
Referrals
Competitors' Clients
Similar directory lists
Compiled broker lists

The closer a potential customer is to you and your organization, the better prospect they are for your marketing efforts.

Branding
Branding is the buzzword today in the area of marketing and advertising. Everyone is talking about branding as if it were a new concept just discovered. In fact, branding has been around as long as advertising has been because it is essentially another aspect of creating your niche or position. A "brand" is just what it sounds like—the thing that sets you apart and by which you want to be known. However, branding nor-

mally is used to convey a broader sense of identity than a USP does. Branding is used by major corporations, universities, and others who have a long history and who anticipate a long future. It incorporates the concept of positioning, but also encompasses the creation of customer loyalty, product or company identity over the long haul, and delivery on promises.

A brand can be communicated through the use of a tagline or a slogan that portrays the image or perception that you want your company to represent. However, it is not a one-time-only slogan; it must be tied into the very essence of the business. In the consumer world, an example of powerful branding is Nike, whose name has come to represent quality athletic shoes for the contemporary athlete. Nike's "Just Do It" campaign illustrates that for a company with a long history and strong brand, the USP can be somewhat ambiguous. However, for most career development practitioners, unless you work for a company with a strong identity, such as IBM or a major university, you will want to work at building your branding over time and use a simple and clear USP in your advertising and promotions.

There are dozens of definitions and descriptions of branding. One inclusive definition refers to six "P"s or components of branding: These are positioning, packaging, promotion, persistence, persuasion, and performance. This definition makes it clear that there are many aspects to developing a brand. Effective branding is comprehensive. As this definition illustrates, it covers many aspects of the business or delivery of services from the positioning and promotions all the way through to performance. Branding is closely tied to the core strategy or identity of the company or the individual making the offer. A tagline, or brand, of a company that does not deliver on its promises is just an empty slogan or promise, not a true brand.

Principle 3: Promote Benefits, Not Features

Any beginning marketing or advertising course will include an introduction to the concept of Benefits vs. Features. This concept applies to the positioning of the product or service and to how it is presented to customers. Stating benefits in your marketing and promotional materials means communicating how your offering will be advantageous, or beneficial, to the customer. A feature, on the other hand, simply relates what the characteristic is.

Using benefits instead of features is related to the customer focus of marketing discussed earlier. Effective marketing not only indicates the features of a product or service, it also shows how those features can be of use to the customer.

You vs. Us

To create marketing materials that use benefits, it helps to take yourself out of your own role as a career development specialist and to place yourself in the role of the potential customer. That means reversing your orientation from "us" and what "we have to offer" and, instead, focusing on "you," the customer, and what the customer wants or needs. How many times have you seen promotional material that focuses on what we have to offer? This is a sign that whoever developed the piece didn't have an understanding of this basic marketing concept. Effective marketing replaces the "we" approach (e.g., why we are so wonderful, what our history is), with a "you" approach that indicates what you will get out of doing business with us. This allows the marketer to place emphasis on the things that will be of importance to the customer and to answer the type of questions a customer may have. These basic customer questions include:

- Is this relevant to me?
- What will I get out of this?
- How will this help me?

The first rule of advertising and promotional copywriting is to turn product features into benefits. Using benefits will make what you have to say more relevant to your intended audience, and it will help you to pinpoint what you need to do to address your audience's needs.

Below are some examples of how features can be turned into benefits for some career development–related offerings. The easiest way to do this is to make a list of the features of what you are marketing, and then write a list of the benefits of each feature. Doing this exercise will force you to think in specific terms about what you are offering and how it will benefit customers. Each time you make a new offering, it will be helpful to complete this exercise. Even seasoned advertising copywriters make a list of benefits to their intended customers before they begin writing. One way I've incorporated this technique into my promotional writing is to write this list out first, take a break, and then return later to be sure that every major feature has a benefit attached to it. So, take a step back to look at what you've written, pretend you are your prospect, and ask yourself if you've answered the question, "What will I get out of this?"

Example: Workshop

Feature: Small group—10–15 attendees are expected
Benefit: Personalized attention and networking opportunities in an intimate small-group setting

Feature: Held one block from the Lowell Center on University of Wisconsin–Madison's campus
Benefit: Within easy walking distance—you'll walk right along the shore of beautiful Lake Monona

Example: Portfolio

Feature: 10 pocket pages included
Benefit: No more searching for lost papers! This system lets you store papers in one convenient spot

Feature: 14 tabbed dividers in different colors
Benefit: It's easy to sort and find materials using the 14 brightly colored tabs

Appeal to Emotions or Desires

Effective advertising appeals to a customer's emotion or desire at some level. In consumer advertising, it is easy to isolate what instinct or desire an advertisement is targeting. Everything from cars to shaving lotions is advertised through commercials that appeal to sex, money, or power. The same principle, appealing to a desire or emotion, is also effective in business-to-business, education, and career development-related marketing. Think about how your service or product might appeal to the emotions or desires of your audience. Often in education and careers-related offerings, these include:

- Desire to get ahead in one's career
- Desire for knowledge
- Desire to be well thought of
- Desire to help others
- Desire to make a meaningful contribution

It is generally not recommended to use a negative emotion or appeal in advertising because it may turn off some readers. However, if done well, you can use an emotion as a way to pull in your reader. Some examples of negative emotions that are often used are fear and pride. In the context of career development, fear could be used in reference to the fear of losing one's job, falling behind in one's field, or being passed over for promotion. Your job as a marketer of careers-related products or services is to figure out what the main appeal to your audience is, and then to use that appeal in your marketing and promotional efforts to grab attention. When using knowledge about what attracts your audience in this way, you draw on the psychographic information uncovered in your customer profile. The perception of what appeals to your audience can be used in a number of ways to strengthen your advertising and promotions.

Here are some examples of advertising phrases that could be used when promoting careers-related products or services. The emotion or desire that is addressed in each example is indicated in parentheses.

- Help your clients help themselves (helping others)
- Are you tired of being passed over for promotions? (fear)
- Jump start your career (desire to get ahead)
- Get the tools you need to get ahead (self-empowerment, career advancement)

Of course, there are many creative ways that you can address your audience's interests in your marketing and promotional materials and campaigns. Once you have determined some of the primary appeals of your target audience, you can begin experimenting with ways to incorporate them into your outreach activities.

Principle 4: Promotional Writing is Different

Often the hardest people to teach about advertising and promotional writing are English teachers, followed by anyone with a high educational level. That is because the rules of grammar taught in school and practiced in research and educational environments do not apply to this type of writing. In fact, many of the things you learned in school should be tossed out when it comes to writing text (called "copy") for a brochure, flyer, advertising e-mail, or Web site.

One rule that does apply to promotional writing is to be clear and consistent. It must be quickly evident what your message is. The simpler the language, the more readable and effective your marketing materials will be. Long, wordy, highly descriptive language has no place in promotional writing. Here are some of the fundamental principles of advertising and promotional writing:

- Use clear, concise language.
- Simple words are better than complex ("use" instead of "usage," "think" instead of "ponder"). This applies even with a highly educated audience.
- Use short, pithy sentences. ("Just do it.")
- Use active, not passive, language.

- Avoid abbreviations, jargon, and acronyms.
- Mix short sentences up with longer ones (makes it easier to read).
- Partial sentences are allowed, even encouraged. ("Easy to adapt." "Ideal for adult learners.")
- Don't be afraid to use the word "you." ("You won't find a better way to stay current.")
- Create a sense of urgency. ("Call today! Spaces are limited.")
- Keep punctuation simple (avoid semicolons, colons, and all unnecessary commas).

Some of the worst promotional copy I've seen has been written by the most knowledgeable and educated professionals. That is because they used long sentences, complex terminology, and acronyms to the point where it was not at all clear what was being said. Simple and clear writing is always preferred in marketing, even if your audience is made up of Ph.D.s, educational leaders, or researchers. Like everyone else, these people are busy, and they will not take the time to decipher your promotional message if its meaning is not readily apparent.

Clever is Not Always Better

Chances are, you have no trouble recalling a television commercial or billboard you saw recently that struck you as clever and funny. Some of the most creative minds around today are being used to put together marketing and advertising campaigns that amuse and attract consumers. However, for those of us in educational and careers-related marketing, humor should be approached with caution.

How to Advertise by Ken Roman and Jane Maas, one of classic books written on advertising, states, "The only problem is people laugh at the joke and forget the product." Effective advertising pulls in the potential customer or client by addressing one of their concerns or interests, and its message must be clear and understandable. Unlike cartoons in the *New Yorker*, or multimillion dollar commercials that air during the Super Bowl, marketing and advertising created by career development professionals must get to the point quickly and state the benefits clearly. Think about how long you take to glance at a poster on a bulletin board in your office building or the amount of time you spend each day deciding which e-mails to read. People are busy and will not take the time to decipher a confusing message. You only have a few seconds to grab attention or lose it. So, be clever if you can be, but do so only if you are not forfeiting the true message.

Content: Put Yourself in the Prospect's Shoes

Early in my career as a copywriter, I worked with a wonderful mentor who had been coaching promotional writers for decades. One of the techniques he taught me has remained with me over the years, and I still use it today. We still used typewriters instead of personal computers back then, and I was told that when I sat down at the typewriter I should picture in my mind an audience member and write to that person as if I was talking to her. Since I was writing fund-raising letters for a nonprofit organization, I formed a mental image of my typical prospect, a 30-something professional woman who liked to support worthwhile causes, and I wrote directly to her. In this way, I was able to address her concerns and answer her questions in a natural, easy manner. This technique is a wonderful tool that I recommend to everyone who thinks they cannot write like a marketer. Simply talk through your keyboard to your audience member, and you will naturally use simple language that will be readable and easily understood.

Another aspect of putting yourself in your prospect's shoes is to consider what questions your prospect will have and answer them. The information you provide will depend upon what product or service you are promoting. When you are putting together a marketing piece such as a Web page, a brochure, or an e-mail, check to be sure that all the important questions a prospect has are covered. These may include:

- Is this for me?
- What will I get out of this?
- Is this a reputable group (or individual)?
- What is the date? time? cost?
- Is credit available?
- Will this help me on the job? How?
- What topics are covered?
- How can I get more information?
- How do I register or purchase?
- What is the deadline?
- Why should I attend (or buy) this one instead of another?
- Is this worth the money for what I will get?

It is essential that any and all marketing pieces contain full contact information for you and your organization. If you are sending a number of materials in the mail (such as a letter, a brochure and a bookmark all together in one package), make certain that each piece contains your name, phone number, e-mail, and full contact information. Often recipients set aside materials to review later and those materials may become separated from the rest. Having contact information on each piece ensures that people have your information at their fingertips.

Be certain that systems are set up to handle any contacts that are generated by your marketing materials. If you put a phone number on a poster or brochure, make sure that someone will be there to answer the phone when someone calls. Nothing discredits your organization and frustrates customers more than not being able to reach someone when they call in to get information, make a purchase, or register for an event, and find that no one is there. This is part of the "back end" of your marketing efforts, and it includes what happens after the initial outreach when potential clients or customers begin responding.

Principle 5: Marketing is Fluid

Because marketing revolves around knowing and meeting the needs of customers, it is important that anyone who does marketing maintains the ability to respond to the changing needs of the audience. The most successful marketing hinges on the ability to see a need as it is first emerging and to respond quickly to fulfill that need. If you doubt this, consider the rise of companies and products such as Microsoft, YouTube, or even products such as bottled water or disposable diapers. In each case, someone saw a need in the marketplace and seized the opportunity to fill it. Naturally, a part of being flexible and able to respond to customer needs quickly is the ability to stay on top of what those needs are. This is why career development practitioners are ideally situated to market their own products and services. As a professional in your field, you already are in tune with what the needs of your audience are, and you are in a position to develop the resources to fill those needs. If you are new to the field, then a great way to gain knowledge of your customers is to read papers and books, attend seminars and conferences, and develop a network of individuals in the field whom you can contact regularly to find out what is new and current.

For individuals who work in large organizations, it can be difficult to respond quickly to market changes due to bureaucracy and slow-moving processes. There are ways you can respond to your market if you work in a large organization or institution; however, it will be more difficult for you to seize new opportunities quickly. That is why we most often see fresh, new approaches growing out of small, entrepreneurial groups rather than out of large companies where one can lose touch with one's customers.

Principle 6: Keep it Simple

As a former advertising copywriter, I find it difficult to admit to one basic truth of marketing and advertising: The way a marketing piece *looks,* how it is designed, may be just as important as what it *says.*

This is an unfortunate truth for anyone who's ever worked on a committee where hours were spent mulling over just the right way to state something in printed materials. The reason why words are less important than the look of a piece is that *no one will ever get around to reading your material if it is hard to follow or to read.* When someone first glances at any kind of communication tool—an e-mail, a letter, a brochure, a Web site—the person's eye will naturally gravitate towards large type, white spaces, and photos. One doesn't have to be a professional designer to know that how things look on the page can invite or deter readability.

Focus on Readability

Here are a few simple concepts to incorporate into marketing and promotional materials. They apply to both print and electronic formats.

Break up blocks of copy. Large blocks of text are hard to read. They are hard on the eye, and they tire the reader out or, worse, make them think it's too much work to read. Instead, make liberal use of white space. Use short paragraphs to break up long blocks of copy. In promotional writing, it is perfectly acceptable—and often a great technique—to use one-line paragraphs.

Choose readable typefaces. Fancy or sophisticated fonts have their place—and that place is on a wedding invitation, not a brochure. Use simple, readable fonts in all advertising materials. It is a proven fact that *serif* typefaces (those with extra lines on the letters) are easier on the eye when used in long text blocks than *sans-serif* typefaces (those without the extra little lines). If you find that hard to believe, take a look at any textbook and you will see that it employs a serif typeface.

Fonts that are ideal for large blocks of copy include New Century Schoolbook and Times New Roman. It is becoming more popular to use sans-serif typefaces such as Arial and Helvetica. Just keep in mind that for long blocks of text, a serif typeface is still more readable.

Font size and color. The eyesight of the average person begins to decrease at the age of 40. That means that if your audience includes anyone age 40 or over,

you need to pay attention to font size, so do not go any smaller than 12 points. Use any type smaller and you will begin to decrease readability. Likewise, keep in mind the color of your type and the background color. Blocks of type should always be in black, or at least a very dark blue or brown. Save other colors for use in headlines and as accent colors to draw attention to a portion of your document, Web page, or e-mail that you want to emphasize.

Use of colors in layouts. Generally speaking, dark type should be used on a lighter colored background in both printed and electronic communications. This produces the highest level of readability. When the background color becomes too dark, it is hard to distinguish the type from the background, and the reader gives up. Blocks of type should never be reversed out of a dark background (i.e., white type on a black background). In small doses, this is an acceptable format when one wants to call attention to a short phrase, such as a short title. When you want to grab attention or indicate urgency, red is the preferred second ink color, proven to be the strongest for attracting attention and promoting action. Examples of this abound: Stop signs are red; overdue bills are marked "Urgent" in red.

Direct the eye where you want it to go. The most obvious way to call attention to headlines is to set them in large type. Using a different typeface, or an accent color, can also allow you to direct attention where you want it. You can put boxes around areas you want to emphasize or put shading behind an area that you want to set apart. Remember that anything with a shaded background will be less readable than text on a white background. However by using other elements, such as larger or bolder type, you can emphasize areas as well. Leaving white space around a title or a block of text will draw the reader's eye to the white space and, subsequently, to the content in the area that is surrounded by it.

Use callouts, captions, diagrams, and graphs. *Callouts* (or *pullquotes*) are parts of the text that you pull out of the rest of the information and put in quotation marks in larger type. Captions are lines of text that you put by a photo. Callouts and captions are always read, and they will be read before the main body of the text because they draw the eye. Graphs, tables, diagrams, and charts draw the eye and emphasize content that can be displayed clearly and simply in this format. These elements also can serve to break up layouts that contain a lot of text and information. A crammed, confusing diagram or chart however, will have the opposite effect and will serve to confuse the reader.

Although every project is different, the diagram below represents the readability for variables of layout and design in a marketing piece that will be true in most cases. Items closer to the top on the readability scale are those that will usually be read first by the user.

Diagram D. Progression of High to Low Readability

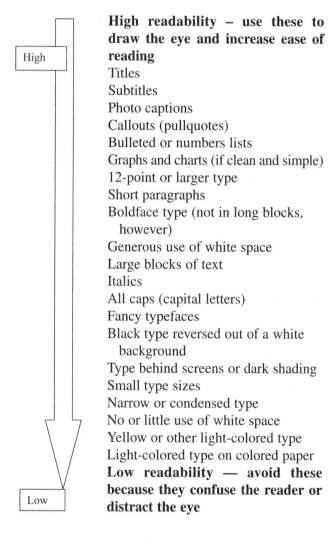

High readability – use these to draw the eye and increase ease of reading
Titles
Subtitles
Photo captions
Callouts (pullquotes)
Bulleted or numbers lists
Graphs and charts (if clean and simple)
12-point or larger type
Short paragraphs
Boldface type (not in long blocks, however)
Generous use of white space
Large blocks of text
Italics
All caps (capital letters)
Fancy typefaces
Black type reversed out of a white background
Type behind screens or dark shading
Small type sizes
Narrow or condensed type
No or little use of white space
Yellow or other light-colored type
Light-colored type on colored paper
Low readability — avoid these because they confuse the reader or distract the eye

Principle 7: Use Techniques Proven to Work

Marketing is always changing to keep pace with customers' needs, lifestyles, and desires. If you pay attention to television advertising, you will notice that advertising trends come and go. For example, for a while you may see a trend where companies advertise using short video-like clips set to music, followed sev-eral months later by everyone switching to using short "storylike" vignettes. There are some things, however, that will not change. These are the basic elements of advertising that are universal, and which are proven to work over and over no matter what the current technology or latest marketing trend. Many of the concepts behind these proven-effective techniques, such as customer orientation and simplicity, have already been discussed.

One thing I've seen many times in my years as a marketer is that what people *say* they will purchase and what they *actually* purchase are not the same. Ask most people what they think about the cost of your service, and nine times out of ten they will tell you it is too expensive. Tracking what works in advertising and marketing has become a complicated science. So you can benefit from the experience of others by incorporating techniques that have been proven to work in advertising and promotional ventures. Below are some additional techniques and tips that can be used to promote career development services and resources.

Grab Attention Fast

Consider how you open your mail when you get home at the end of the day. You first sort through and pull out the important mail such as bills or personal letters, and glance through the rest, tossing them into the garbage. You probably spend less than a second or two before you decide whether to toss or keep a piece of mail.

Your customers do the same thing, whether you are reaching out to them by mail at home or the office, by e-mail, or via a Web site. You have just a few seconds to draw their interest to your brochure or letter. For e-mails, that time may be just a split second. In that amount of time, you must attract the attention of the prospect, and convince him or her to open the e-mail, read the brochure, or peruse the Web site. To grab attention, you must decide what will make your promotion stand out among all the others that your prospects receive. If you have a relationship with your prospect, it often works to display that relationship up front. For example, if they know your organization, make your organization's name show up as the Sender of the e-mail. Other ideas to draw attention include:

- Ask a question (it must be one they care about answering).
- Make an announcement; show what's new and upcoming.
- Personalize it (people always look at their name).

- Pinpoint a major concern or problem (and show how you will solve it).
- State a benefit up front.
- Start a sentence (for example, on the front of a brochure) …
  … and finish it inside (this pulls the reader in).

Testimonials

Testimonials can contribute credibility to marketing and promotional materials. Potential customers pay attention to what others are saying, so including testimonials from past buyers, leaders your audience may know, or other significant people can help strengthen your message. Consumer marketers often use celebrities to endorse their products, and they do so because it works! The careers-related equivalent of a celebrity endorsement is a quote from a well-known career development author or leader who can speak to the relevancy or quality of your offering.

Should you include the names of the individuals providing your testimonials? If possible, yes. Testimonials that are attributed to a real person are stronger than those that are more ambiguous, such as "past participant." Obtain a signed release from individuals you quote in your marketing materials and keep them on file. It is best to err on the side of being too cautious, so get a signed release when in doubt. Testimonials can be obtained from:

- Prominent people known to the audience, such as leaders in the field, politicians, etc.
- Colleagues and peers of the intended audience
- Past participants or clients

The more specific and detailed the statement, the stronger the testimonial. Choose statements that point to the specific benefits you want to convey. When marketing a national conference on career development, for example, I use testimonials such as these to emphasize what I am saying elsewhere in the material:

- "pertinent topics"
- "very well organized"
- "practical ideas I know I can use"
- "preconference session was excellent, tours also great!"
- "exceptional presenters, useful information, and outstanding accommodations!!!"
- "you took excellent care of guests"
- "so much to choose from it was hard to decide"

Here are some examples of the type of effective testimonials attributed to a colleague of the intended audience for a career development training event:

> "This was the best workshop on employability skills I've ever attended—and I've been attending these events for 25 years!"
> Jim Stoughton, Private Career Counselor, Madison, WI

> "I can't say thank you enough. This training changed the way I work every day—I honestly left with two new strategies for working with my hard-to-place clients."
> Jane Worthsmill, Career Advisor, Community College of the Pacific, Seattle, WA

Photos

The general rule of thumb about use of photos in brochures is that it can be effective *if* you choose the right photos, and *if* you are able to produce them well. Using a grainy-looking or fuzzy photo or one that does not well represent your offering is worse than using no photo at all. Photos are useful for creating interest and for breaking up large blocks of text in both print and Web-based promotions.

Photos of people are usually preferred over still shots such as a building, because they generate more interest. People subconsciously relate to the people they see in photos, so choose subjects who are similar in age and lifestyle to your intended audience, and be sure they are presented in a favorable light. They should look like they are happy and are enjoying your program or service. Keep in mind race, gender, age, and ethnicity of your subjects, and be certain that the photos reflect accurately the makeup of your intended audience. Again, be sure that you have a signed release when using photos of people in your marketing.

Consider the quality of the photos you use. Photos that look fine in an online format may be grainy and of poor quality if used for a print project. Disks of stock photos can be purchased for relatively minimal expense if you need photos on a regular basis and are unable to shoot them yourself. If you purchase stock photos, the purchase agreement will often have a time-frame during which the photos can be used.

Building Credibility

People today are constantly subjected to unwanted advertising and marketing messages including spam, junk mail, telemarketing calls, and screen pop-ups. Many of these messages come from fraudulent or less-than-desirable sources. Therefore, it is important to take steps to address the issues of credibility and reliability in your marketing materials. Show that you are with a reputable organization and that what you offer is of top quality. This will strengthen your message and make it stand out from others that are of lesser quality. There are a number of ways to do this.

If you work for a reputable company, organization, or institution, include organizational information in your promotions and advertising mesages. If your organization has its own brand or logo, as do major universities and corporations, build on the strength and loyalty of the brand by including it. This will assure customers that you are not with a disreputable group. On the other hand, if you do not have a larger reputable group with which to associate, then find other means to show that you are credible. These include:

- using testimonials from past customers or others known to your audience,
- mentioning any accreditations or recommendations you have earned,
- indicating historical markers such as how long you've been in business, or
- having a related association provide an endorsement.

When the qualifications of an author or speaker are important to your program, list honors, degrees, recommendations, and related work experience to show that the individual is well qualified. Specific endorsements or information about how this person's expertise has been realized (outcomes of their work) will also increase credibility.

How you do business with your customers, how customer friendly your processes are, and how responsive you are to customers' needs over time, will build credibility as well. If you are using branding, the practices below will assist in presenting you and your organization as one that can be trusted.

- Avoid hype and do not overstate claims in marketing materials.
- Use business-like type fonts and clean layouts on the Web and in printed materials.
- Provide "opt out" options for e-mails and other mailing lists.
- Employ a consistent "family look" to all marketing materials.
- Consistently use a logo or tagline.
- Provide readable and cleanly designed marketing materials as described in this monograph.

Address Objections Head On

Every so often when I am working with career development practitioners, someone presents a marketing challenge that honestly cannot be met. These are cases where someone is working "uphill," trying to convince their prospective audience that they "need" something that the audience does not believe they need, or that they do not want. Remember: The purpose of marketing is to *attract* customers. Generally, it will not be effective if you believe you need to *change your customers' mindset* as part of your advertising.

For example, if you are marketing a booklet on the topic of "How to Enroll in a Two-year Technical College" and your audience is made up of individuals who believe a two-year degree is a waste of time and money (for whatever reason), your marketing efforts will not succeed, no matter how well executed they are. That is because the goal of your marketing efforts cannot be used to change the mindset of your potential customer. Successful marketing must be based on using the knowledge you have of the potential customer—including how they think and perceive things—and designing programs and services around that. That is not to say that you cannot influence your audience once they come to you for your services or programs. But rather, your efforts will be best utilized if you show that you understand your audience and their needs when trying to attract their interest, rather than trying to change them.

Another technique that is proven to work is addressing possible objections up front in your marketing. For example, if you know that the cost of your services is something that will be a concern, find ways to address that concern in your marketing. Rather than ignoring the topic entirely, can you come up with ways to show that it is worth the cost? Maybe you could quote a previous buyer who decided it was well worth the cost, compare the cost to what other competitors are charging, or list all the positive outcomes and benefits and show the value for the cost. Whatever roadblocks exist in your prospects' minds, thinking about how to handle them and addressing them directly can work to strengthen your marketing. Possible objections should also be addressed in the planning stages before you get to promotional activities. If cost is going to be an issue, incorporate that concern into your program planning and try to develop ways to help make the offering affordable. You might, for example, determine to run a half-day workshop instead of a full-day workshop, or decide that you need to find a funding partner before you move ahead on your idea.

Use Specifics, Lists, and Bullets

The liberal use of lists, either numbered or bulleted, pulls the reader in and strengthens marketing copy. Vague concepts are hard to sell, but specific information and content will answer customers' questions and improve response. Lists should be indented, and the white space around them will draw the eye. Likewise, use as many specifics as possible if those specifics will provide valuable information. Lists can be used to present topics, speakers, chapters (of a book or article), sponsors, and many other factors. The use of a list of benefits could be used to strengthen the marketing of a conference in this way:

Here's what you will get by attending this event:

- Ideas you can put to use immediately.
- Opportunity to network with colleagues across the nation.
- More than a dozen in-depth training workshops on key topics.
- Chance to get feedback on your current programs and projects.
- Updates on best practices in the field.

Direct mail letters often serve as great examples of how to use lists and specifics in promotions. Have you ever received a direct mail offer for a book where the entire letter consists of lists of what you will get in the book? Sometimes these letters go on for pages about what is included in the book. Health-related books do this by giving you lists of natural remedies you will find for any illness, or exercises you can do for dozens of reasons to become healthier—all with details to be found only in the book. A lot can be learned about how to market from reading marketing materials such as these and adapting these techniques so they work in the area of career development.

Lessons Learned from Direct Response

As previously mentioned, "direct response" refers to a marketing method (usually mailings but sometimes television commercials and other advertisements) where a *direct, immediate* response is requested. Some examples of direct response promotions are a magazine advertisement that has a coupon to send back, a television "infomercial" with an 800 number to call immediately, or a mailing with a letter and brochure that includes a reply card with a deadline to be returned. This type of promotion can be illustrated as follows:

Direct = goes right to (directly) the target person
Response = requires a response of some kind

Direct response has been called "your sales people in print," and this concept applies to all kinds of print and most electronic marketing methods. When no sales person is talking to a customer, your marketing and promotional material needs to serve as the sales person. That means it must include all the information that would be communicated in a conversation between the sales person and the prospect.

A key point gleaned from the world of direct response is the importance of asking for a response. It is widely known that the main reason people do not give money to nonprofit organizations is because they are not asked. The same applies to any marketing effort. It must be clear what response you are looking for (a phone call, an order, an e-mail inquiry), and it must be clear in your promotions what the prospect needs to do to follow up.

Direct response methods include a way to assess, or measure, the response to the marketing activity. This is what occurs when you call to place an order on the telephone for a catalog item and the representative asks for the code on your mailing label. Having a system to track responses allows direct marketers to determine if a marketing effort is working. Many marketers of careers-related programs will be unable to track responses in this manner; however, some type of evaluation of promotions should be made using information that is obtainable to determine if marketing efforts are effective.

Proofreading

It is a good idea to have two different people review all promotional and marketing materials before they are printed or posted live. The first is someone who is involved in the project and who can review materials for accuracy of the information. This person should review all letters, Web page material, brochures, etc., checking to be sure all the details are accurate.

The second review should be done by someone who is not at all familiar with your product or service. This person should review the information to be sure it includes all the information necessary for a prospect to make a decision or to take further action. It includes not only details such as location, timing, and contact information, but also the "big picture" marketing issues discussed earlier, such as "why should I purchase or attend this one instead of another?" Be sure all dates, phone numbers, and every other small detail is correct. Publicizing materials with any of this vital information missing or incorrect is a big mistake that can seriously affect the outcome of your program.

Chapter 4
Promotions and Publicity on a Budget

If cost is not an object for you in your marketing efforts, then you are lucky. Most practitioners and the organizations they work for have limited budgets and resources with which to work to promote their services. Whether you do some parts of the marketing activities, do all of them yourself, or work as part of a team to get them done, the ideas presented below could be useful to you if you are looking for ways to stretch your promotional dollars.

Marketing activities can range from expensive to inexpensive. The good news is that expensive does not necessarily always mean better. The kind of marketing methods you use, as well as how you use them, will depend largely upon your particular situation in terms of staffing, resources, and technology. If you have a designer to work with and the funds to use a printing company for your brochure, you will have many more options than someone who has no printing budget and who must write, design, and photocopy brochures themselves.

Cost Considerations for Print Promotions

The most expensive marketing pieces are printed by a professional printing company on expensive-looking paper in full color (called four-color or six-color printing, depending on the press used). There are many types of format and techniques that can add pizzazz and style to printed pieces. These include die cutting (cutting out shapes in the paper, foils (a print process that looks like actual foil is attached), fancy accordion folds, and many others. These techniques are expensive. Here are some ways to produce printed materials at reduced cost.

Cost-Cutting Ideas

Avoid odd sizes. The most inexpensive way to lay out a brochure is to use a standard 8 ½ x 11" paper. This size paper can be folded into thirds horizontally into a standard three-panel brochure. If you are using a printer, ask for advice on choosing standard paper sizes. Any time you choose a paper size that is non-standard for the press you are using, you will pay extra. A standard 8 ½ x 11" sheet can also be cut into

smaller sizes to produce bookmarks or smaller flyers, with several produced from just one sheet of paper.

Use two instead of four colors. Four-color (or six-color) printing is expensive. To cut costs, use two colors. A multicolor effect can be achieved with the creative use of two colors and the use of screens and shading. Two-color printing for brochures should generally be black, for the main text, with a second color for highlights and contrast. The least expensive way to print is one color only (black).

Use simple folds. Choose a simple three-panel fold when designing a brochure. Any time you add complicated folds, or increase the number of folds in a piece, the cost will increase. Also keep in mind the marketing principle of simplicity: Keep your materials simple and easy to open and to follow. A legal-size sheet of paper folds nicely into a four-panel brochure.

Use self-mailers and postcards. If you are doing mailings that include one or several pieces in an envelope, you need to add the cost of the envelope to your expenses. To save money, see if the piece can be designed as an economical self-mailer instead. Postcards are also a more inexpensive way to get information out if you do not need a lot of space to explain your product or service, because you will save on postage and paper.

Photocopy flyers on colored paper. When you need just a small quantity of flyers or brochures, consider photocopying them on colored paper on a regular copier. This is far less expensive than doing a small run on a printing press. This inexpensive technique is very effective when you choose an attention-grabbing paper color, such as golden or neon green. Remember to keep the paper light in color; black ink on dark paper colors is hard to read.

Use a color copier. For general copying, color copies are considered expensive. But when it comes to producing marketing materials, using a color copier for a small quantity of flyers, posters, or brochures can produce a very professional-looking piece for a fraction of the cost of regular printing on a press.

Additional Factors to Consider

Design considerations. New computer programs suitable for design are being developed regularly. If you are not using a professional designer and doing the layout and design yourself, there are a number of programs to choose from, and a variety of templates for simple design that can yield an attractive piece.

Paper selection. The paper on which brochures, letters, and flyers are printed makes a big difference in the look and feel of the piece. In general, heavier paper stock is more expensive than light-weight paper. Coated, glossy, or semiglossy paper is a better choice for reproduction of photos, but they are also more expensive. A linen or other quality stock will give printed material a higher quality feel, but it can be harder to read text on paper that is textured.

Lists. Mailing and e-mail lists that are compiled and maintained to a high degree of quality are essential to most marketing. The list that you use to e-mail or to mail your promotional materials is far more important than what the promotional copy says. That's because you can send out an e-mail with a minor typo or mediocre copy and still get some response—but if you send it to wrong addresses or to the wrong target group, you will get no response.

If you are with a large organization or have enough monetary resources, you may consider purchasing mailing and e-mail lists. Buying lists is extremely expensive. However, everyone who does marketing should put considerable time and effort into compiling and maintaining their own lists. A customer list that is well maintained is critical to marketing efforts and is often referred to as an organization's "bread and butter." That is because current and past customers are always going to be the best performing lists. The second type of list you should develop is a prospect list. This could include competitors' customers, inquiries, and others you have added to your contacts over time.

Cost Considerations for Electronic Promotions

The simplest of electronic marketing methods, sending e-mails from your personal computer, is also the least expensive. When compared to promotional methods where there is printing or copying involved, it is less costly to e-mail. If you send a notice or announcement to your address book of contacts and colleagues, it is basically free. Once you begin adding compiled lists or purchased lists and sending large amount of e-mails, costs begin to be added.

A variety of electronic methods are being used to promote programs and services, and this is an area where I receive a lot of questions from practitioners. Some of these methods are discussed in the following chapter, including the costs involved. Which methods you choose to use will depend upon your particular needs, your budget, and your staff and resources.

Chapter 5
What About E-Marketing?

The electronic age has presented marketers with a range of new promotional methods to reach audiences that are computer literate and Web savvy. The elementary marketing concepts already discussed—customer focus, simplicity of design, and the promotion of benefits—will not change when using electronic or high-tech marketing methods. These principles will not be altered any time in the future either, as they are based on the psychology of what attracts attention and what works in advertising. There are some specific considerations to observe when using these newer marketing methods, and they are discussed here.

Electronic marketing may make sense in your overall marketing plan, in situations such as these:

- When you need to save money
- When you don't have time, staff, or resources to do print marketing
- When it's a short message
- When you need to reach a lot of people quickly
- When you acquired those people through electronic means

Web Marketing

Web sites range from simple sites with just one page to complex sites with multiple pages. A Web site can be considered a marketing vehicle because it is used to reach both prospects and current or past customers. Prospects may visit your Web page via methods that include doing a Web search for related topics, following a link from another site, or responding to a promotion that mentions the site. Customers and past customers already know about your site and will come back if the site offers something of value and if it is updated on a regular basis to provide information about new developments or programs.

The necessity of using simplicity in design applies to Web pages just as it does to printed promotional materials. A Web site must be clean and easy to read and follow. The organization of information may be even more important in Web design than it is on a brochure. It must be easy for the Web visitor to locate what he wants from the home page and easy to navigate through the site. Make sure that type is large enough and that color backgrounds do not compete with the text. Web pages should incorporate the use of white space and avoid large blocks of text copy. Photos can be used for interest, and buttons and links can be used to help organize material and move the reader to the next page. Just as the front of a brochure should be worded to encourage the reader to open up to the next page, so a Web site home page should be designed to encourage the reader to click further for more information. Once again, keep in mind that people are busy. They will not wait for pages, tables, or documents to download, but will click out if things take too long to come up. Anything you put up on a Web site should be tested on a variety of machines and with different browsers to ensure that quick downloading is possible.

When designing Web pages, it is tempting to use the latest techniques because they are fun and are perceived to add interest. However, it is best to avoid any technology that may confuse or distract the audience from your message. Flashing symbols, scrolling text, and other high-profile treatments can annoy, rather than attract, readership. Remember the purpose of a Web page is to provide information and attract interest, not to win awards.

Web pages should be designed to be accessible to individuals with disabilities. Tables, photos, diagrams, attached files including Word or PDF documents, and all other parts of the page should be set up so that they are accessible. One of the most important parts of making Web marketing effective is to be sure that information and contacts are current and that links are working properly. If you lead a prospect to your Web site, but the link for more information is not working, then you have lost a potential customer. Web sites, when properly set up and maintained, are a good way to get information out to both current and prospective customers. Providing regular updates or news on your Web site encourages past customers to keep coming back to find out what is new.

E-mails

Using e-mails for marketing and promotions offers speed and convenience. You can compose an e-mail at your desk and send it out to arrive within minutes to your intended audience. E-mails are the most inexpensive way to market, requiring nothing more than a computer and an e-mail account. On the receiver's end, e-mails can be read immediately or stored, categorized, and archived in the recipient's files for future reference.

As with other types of outreach efforts, simplicity and readability are essential ingredients in the creation of an e-mail that will achieve its goal. E-mails can be sent in simple text format, in an html format where graphics and design elements can be included, or in a text format with a link to an html format or Web page for those readers who prefer that format.

As e-mail usage has grown, e-mail advertisers face increasing challenges. First is the development of new and more sophisticated blockers and filters on the recipient's account. More and more e-mails are being labeled as spam by these blockers and filters, and this trend is going to continue. This makes it difficult for e-mails to get through to the intended person. In the U.S., the Can-Spam legislation of 2004 makes it a requirement that "opt out" options be provided in commercial e-mail offers. (This legislation does allow spam e-mails with the permission of the user.) If you have a previous relationship with the customer, this "opt out" requirement does not apply. This legislation is easy to comply with if you ask the people you send e-mails to inform you if they do not want to receive e-mail messages from you. You will need to keep a list of these e-mail prospects to avoid sending e-mails to them in the future.

The guidelines below may be used to assist in developing effective e-mails for marketing and increase the likelihood that they will reach the intended recipient.

Avoid looking like spam. Make your e-mails look like personal mail. Use your own name or the name of someone the recipient will recognize as the sender. If your organization is known by the prospect, the organization can be used as the sender.

Do not use attachments and large graphics. Most people will not click into attachments because of the possible danger of carrying a virus to their machine, assuming the e-mail gets through a filter or blocker to begin with. In addition, many e-mails with graphics will either not get through filters or, for graphics, may not display quickly or properly.

Be aware of format changes. When you design e-mails, keep in mind that what shows on your screen may not be the same as what will show on the recipient's screen. Review how the e-mail will display on different browsers and systems before you send it out by conducting some tests beforehand.

Carefully craft the subject line. Most people will look at the sender first and then the subject line to decide if they will read the e-mails in their in box. Make sure that your subject line captures the interest of your reader, using the promotional writing tips discussed earlier. The subject line in an e-mail is equivalent to the envelope in a mailing: Your goal is to get it opened before it gets thrown into the trash.

Avoid commercial advertising terms. Many filters will automatically block out common advertising words, so it is best to avoid them. These include: free, improved, new, offer, money, save, win, and similar common advertising terms. Though these terms may get through in some cases, it is best to err on the side of safety so that more e-mails will get through to your recipient.

Make it easy to read. E-mails are usually scanned, so make it brief and to the point. Include the essential information you need, but be sure there is either a link to a Web page with details, or an e-mail address to use to request more information. Paragraphs in e-mails should be short. It is far better to have many short paragraphs than one long one which will likely not be read.

Critique and test. After you compose your e-mail, send it to yourself first. See how it will look in the recipient's in box and consider whether it will get opened or not. Check to see if all critical information is included and if there is any way you can improve the message. Be sure to run spell check on all e-mails before you send them out.

Limit the number of e-mails sent at once. Some filters and blocks will immediately label e-mails sent to groups as spam, so divide large lists into smaller groups before sending them.

As e-mail promotion use continues to grow and evolve, a whole industry of e-mail lists and e-mail technology through commercial vendors is taking shape. Compiled e-mail lists are now available for purchase, just as they are for mailings. These compiled lists, like their mailing counterparts, will be less likely to yield positive response compared to other types of lists where you are closer to the prospect. E-mail vendors are also available to design and deliver your e-mail message, with computers programmed to send just a few at a time, allowing more e-mails to get through filters. These services, as expected, are costly and may not fit in the budget for the majority of careers-related practitioners at this time.

Electronic Mailing Lists

Electronic mailing lists are electronic groups of people who share a similar interest. There are electronic mailing lists for nearly every interest available, including counselors and educators, delineated by geographic location, practice area, or curriculum interest. Electronic mailing lists can be a great resource for career development marketers. Electronic mailing lists allow members to post messages to a large group at the same time and are a good way to reach your target audience. By sending an e-mail to an electronic mailing list of counselors with an interest in careers, you can reach a lot of people with just one message.

Most electronic mailing lists have two addresses for posting a message: (1) the address that members use to send mail that gets distributed to everyone on the list, and (2) the address that is used to send commands (such as "subscribe" or "unsubscribe") to the list administrator. You must join the electronic mailing list before you are able to post a message to the group. Each electronic mailing list has its own flavor, amount of usage by members, and rules for posting. Not all electronic mailing lists allow marketing information to be posted, so be sure that it is allowed before you send a marketing message to any electronic mailing list you join. Even if you cannot post marketing material, you can still join appropriate electronic mailing lists to get other information that can be used in your program planning and marketing, such as what the hot topics are and what problems your customers are facing.

Some of the benefits of marketing to electronic mailing lists include:

- Won't be labeled as spam
- Can write your message as informational (not promotional)
- Will be targeted to the specific group you want to reach
- No cost
- Quickest way to reach a group
- Can help in relationship building

Podcasts and Webinars

It is becoming more and more common to hear about both podcasts and Webinars, or e-seminars, being used for a variety of purposes. These newer technologies may be methods to consider if your audience includes younger individuals or those who use newer technologies on a regular basis. Webinars are available in a number of formats that vary in delivery cost and format, with options that include live camera showing the presenter(s), still camera only, and no camera at all (i.e., a PowerPoint presentation that is broadcast with sound over phone lines). Podcasts are broadcast programs or messages that can be accessed by the listener with an I-pod or similar listening device. Any of these technologies can be used to build the relationship you have with current customers or reach out to new prospects in much the same way that print or electronic newsletters do. For example, you can develop a Webinar that provides career development information to the audience and then follow up with the participants with further offers. Used in this way, a Webinar or podcast can help with branding by establishing your organization as an information "expert."

When to Use Electronic Marketing

Depending on method, electronic marketing may be especially suited for promotions in certain types of situations. The chart on the following pages shows some of the reasons for promotional activity and which electronic marketing methods may be suitable.

Table 2. When to Use Electronic Marketing vs. Print (brochure)

	Send an email message	Put up a web page	Post on an electronic mailing list	Post on an e-calendar	Do a webcast or podcast	Send a brochure in the mail
Need to reach as many people as possible	√	√	√	√		
Timing is essential to my message (has a tight deadline)	√		√	√		
Low cost is a top priority	√		√	√		
Information should be referred to over and over by recipient	√	√			√	√
Purpose is to announce a new workshop	√	√	√	√		√
Message has a very narrow audience	√		√		√	√
Must include a registration form	√	√	√			√
Purpose is to build relationships with potential customers	√	√	√		√	
Need to portray a strong, credible image	√	√	√		√	√
Want to reach my current customers/ students only	√					√
Want to find out if there's interest in my idea	√		√			

	Send an email message	Put up a web page	Post on an electronic mailing list	Post on an e-calendar	Do a webcast or podcast	Send a brochure in the mail
Need information back ASAP	√		√			
Message must be personalized to an individual	√					
Purpose is to provide information on a new development	√	√	√		√	√
Want to have people save the date for my event	√		√	√		
Have a poorly maintained database of names/lists		√	√	√		
Timing is not as important as the content of the message		√			√	√
Have very limited staff and resources for promotional activity	√		√	√		
Have a very broad audience		√		√		
This message's content is part of an ongoing department series	√	√			√	√

Additional E-Marketing Pointers

Here are some additional ways to market electronically. All of these are cost free and easy to implement.

- Join electronic mailing lists and e-groups.
- Post on relevant association Web pages and event calendars.
- Compile your own e-mail lists.
  - Set up your computer to save incoming e-mails.
  - Get attendee and association lists.
  - Get referrals from colleagues and others.
- Use your Web site to get contact names.
- Link from related Web sites.

Future Methods

It is hard to say what new electronic methods the future will bring, though there certainly will be more options available for marketers to use. Some of the electronic technologies discussed here will become less costly to use, and some will grow more ineffective as they become overused by marketers and others. What is certain is that the general principles of simplicity, clarity, and purposefulness will continue to apply to whatever electronic methods of marketing practitioners use now or in the future. A Web search for terms such as "marketing" or "electronic marketing" will yield a large number of Web sites, blogs, books, and other resources that you can use to stay current with the ever-changing technologies that can be used for marketing.

Conclusion

Successful marketing does not end with one event or a fixed period of time. The best marketing efforts require that the marketer keep eyes and ears open for new opportunities at all times. Effective marketing is a comprehensive and ongoing effort that includes research, program development, marketing strategy or plan, promotional activities, and customer feedback and assessment. While developing a marketing plan is a linear process, the whole process of marketing is best understood as a circular, comprehensive continuum where each part feeds important information into the other parts and where they all are integrated.

By developing a thorough knowledge of one's customers and keeping up with the trends and issues that are important to them, marketers will be in the best position to develop and deliver programs and services that will be of true value to their clients and customers. This knowledge of the customer must become integrated into every portion of the planning, development, and implementation of careers-related services and programs.

Although much of marketing is simple common sense, even those who do not have an intuitive understanding of the essence of marketing can learn to create and disseminate information about their services that will be effective in attracting customers and clients. Basic principles of marketing that do not change over time or with the application used include: (1) customer orientation, (2) creating your niche, (3) using promotional writing techniques, (4) promoting benefits, (5) being flexible, (6) focusing on readability, and (7) using what has been proven to work.

Creating promotional materials for print or electronic formats involves writing directly to the customer and answering the customer's question, "What will I get out of this?" Proven promotional writing techniques include:

- Be short and to-the-point.
- Break up blocks of copy.
- Use simple words and layouts.
- Focus on the customers' needs, not on you or your program.
- Build credibility.
- Use white space and subheads.
- Include necessary information.
- Write clearly, not cleverly.

Looking Ahead

The only certainty about future marketing methodology is that the methods will continue to evolve and change. As technology changes, and as legislation related to electronic and other methods evolves, career development marketers will need to find new ways to effectively reach clients, customers, and prospects.

Regardless of changes in technology, marketing will always revolve around the process and principles outlined in this monograph. The customer will always come first, developing programs and services around meeting customers' needs will always be the goal, and using fundamental marketing theory and proven marketing techniques will always set the career development marketer on the road to success.

Appendices

A. Possible Components of the Marketing Mix

B. Press Release Tips

C. Template of Basic Marketing Plan

D. Sample Excel Worksheet for Estimating
   Expenses and Income

E. "Paint a Customer Profile" Worksheet

Appendix A
Possible Components of the Marketing Mix

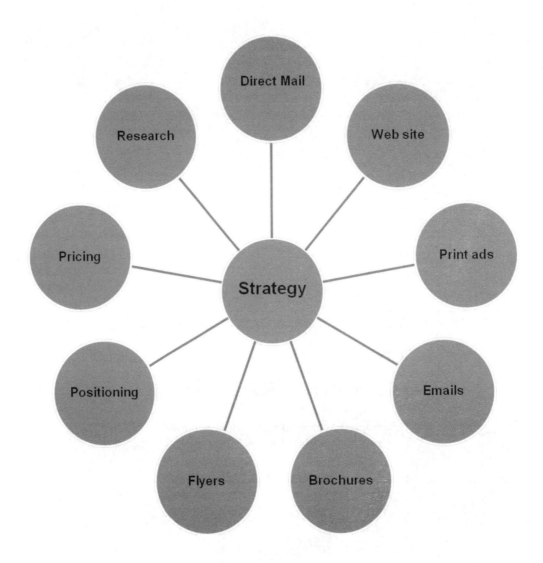

Appendix B
Press Release Tips
for Print and Electronic Media

1. Find the *news* in what you are writing about and use it. There has to be a news angle in order for it to be considered newsworthy.

2. Use factual language—do not use sales or promotional tone or terms.

3. Answer Who, What, When, Where, and How.

4. Use a strong lead that emphasizes the news angle and that pulls in the reader.

5. Put your most important information up front and less important information at the end (editors often cut items for space).

6. Include your name and full contact information.

7. If you are with a company, institution, or organization, give a brief summary of what the organization does.

8. Write clearly and succinctly.

9. Include a release date on your press release.

10. Develop a list of appropriate news sources (where you will have a connection with the readership)—and send the news release to the correct ones.

11. Finally, *don't call* or follow up with news sources. This can annoy them and might cause them to not run your release. Editors will contact you if they need further information.

Appendix C
Template of Basic Marketing Plan

This template can be copied and used to help you develop and document your marketing plan.

MARKETING PLAN TEMPLATE

Program/Service name:_____

Developed by:_____

Date created:_____

OBJECTIVE: What do I want to achieve?	
WHO: Define my audience	
METHODS: How will I do this?	
WHEN: What is the timeframe or day/time?	
REQUIRED RESOURCES: What people/tools/or other are needed to accomplish this?	
ESTIMATED COSTS: Attach a budget sheet showing cost/income projections	
PROMOTIONS: How will I let my audience know?	
MEASURE OF ACHIEVEMENT/ OUTCOMES: How will I tell if it was successful?	

Appendix D
Sample Excel Worksheet for Estimating Expenses and Income

Workshop Expense/Income Costs (estimated)		
Item	**Cost**	**Comments**
Equipment and Room Expenses		
Room Rental	$75.00	1-day fee
Projector and screen rental	$150.00	1-day fee
Materials for participants		
Binders	$120.00	3.00 each x 40
Copies	$50.00	
Marketing costs		
Mailing & Postage	$900.00	designed as self-mailer
Brochure printing	$650.00	2-color, 3-fold
E-mail campaign	$0	
Course materials		
Instructor materials	$100.00	
Parking costs		
	$160.00	20 persons x $8
Staff and consulting fees		
Designer	$200.00	
Instructor	$300.00	
Total Expenses	**$2,705.00**	
Income		
Registrations income	$3,000.00	estimated 40 x $75
Parking	$160.00	20 persons x $8
Total Income	**$3,160.00**	
Workshop Revenue	**$455.00**	

43

Appendix E
"Paint a Customer Profile" Worksheet

Paint a Profile of Your Audience

Who is My Customer?

Typical Demographics

Age, gender, educational level, place of residency, income, marital status, occupation, rural/urban, access to transportation, type of work environment, ethnicity, lifestyle, and any other factors that paint a picture of your target audience:

_____

_____

_____

_____

_____

_____

_____

Likely Psychographics

Attitudes, predispositions, general attributes, psychological factors that may influence how they perceive your service, product, or event:

_____

_____

_____

_____

_____

_____

_____

Resources

Basics of Advertising and Promotions, Advertising Law. Retrieved July 9, 2003 from http://www.managementhelp.org/ad_prmopt/ad_prmot.htm [no longer accessible].

Chase, L., How to attract traffic to your site using press releases. *Web Digest for Marketers.* Retrieved from http://www.wdfm.com/press-releases.php

Cooper, S., & Heenan, C. (1980). Key elements in workshop design, taken from *Preparing, Designing, Leading Workshops: A Humanistic Approach.* Boston: CBI Publishing. Retrieved August 1, 2003 at http://www2.hawaii.edu/~jharris/wsc/workshop_design_strategies/key_design_elements.html

Eash, E. K. (2006, April). Podcasting 101 for K-12 librarians. *Computers in Libraries,* Vol. 26 No(4). Retrieved from http://www.infotoday.com/cilmag/apr06/Eash.shtml

Eisenberg, B. (2004, September 24). Power persuasive copy to punch up sales. *ClickZ, Advice & Opinions. By & For Marketers.* Retrieved from http://www.clickz.com/showPage.html?page=3412131

Eisenberg, B. (2004, September 10). The five issues that persuade visitors. *ClickZ, Advice & Opinions. By & For Marketers.* Retrieved from http://www.clickz.com/showPage.html?page=3405251

Eisenberg, B. (2001, June 25). It's the customer, stupid. *ClickZ, Advice & Opinions. By & For Marketers.* Retrieved from http://www.clickz.com/showPage.html?page=843281

Eyram, S. (2004, November 2). Building an e-mail marketing database is easier [electronic version]. *Direct Marketing News.* Retrieved from http://www.marketingpower.com/live/content19543C144.php [login required].

Gedney, K. (2004, July 14). Winning subject lines. *ClickZ, Advice & Opinions. By & For Marketers.* Retrieved from http://www.clickz.com/showPage.html?page=3379451

Gedney, K. (2004, September 22). Create personal PR with e-mail. *ClickZ, Advice & Opinions. By & For Marketers.* Retrieved from http://www.clickz.com/experts/em_mkt/b2b_em_mkt/article.php/3410671

How to write a press release. InfoScavenger Communications, Inc. Retrieved from http://www.infoscavenger.com/prtips.htm

Levison, I. Nine ways to write headlines that make money. *The Levinson Letter: Direct Mail, E-mail and Advertising Copywriting.* Retrieved July 11, 2003 from http://www.levison.com/art11.htm [no longer accessible].

Major Methods of Advertising and Promotion. Retrieved July 9, 2003 from http://www.mapnp/org/library/pblc_rel/basics.htm [no longer accessible].

Nielsen, J. (1997, October 1). How users read on the Web. Retrieved from *Alertbox,* http://www.useit.com/alertbox/9710a.html

Petersen, C. (2001, May 1). Writing for a web audience. *IBM developerWorks.* Retrieved July 15, 2003 from http://www-106.ibm.com/developerworks/usability/library/us-writ/ [no longer accessible].

Soltoff, P. (2004, June 28). What e-mail marketers can learn from banner ads. *ClickZ, Advice & Opinions. By & For Marketers.* Retrieved from http://www.clickz.com/showPage.html?page=3372941

Roman, K. & Maas, J. (2003). *How to Advertise* (3rd ed.). New York: Thomas Dunne Books.

Tschabitscher, H. When in doubt, send plain text email, not fancy HTML. Retrieved from *About. com: Email,* http://email.about.com/cs/netiquettetips/qt/et070103.htm

Tschabitscher, H. Ask before you send huge attachments. Retrieved from *About. com: Email,* http://email.about.com/cs/netiquettetips/qt/et021801.htm

United States set to legalize spamming on January 1, 2004 (2003, November 22). *Spamhaus News.* Retrieved from http://www.spamhaus.org/news.lasso?article=150